SENSITIVE TEACHER

A CAREFUL GUIDE TO BECOMING THE IDEAL PARENT

JESSICA E. PEDERSEN

DISCLAIMER

TABLE OF CONTENT

SENSITIVE TEACHER

DISCLAIMER

TABLE OF CONTENT

INTRODUCTION

CHAPTER ONE: INCREDIBLY NICE

CHAPTER TWO: YOIR OBLIGATIONS AND RIGHTS

CHAPTER THREE: IT'S BETTER LATE THAN NEVER!

CHAPTER FOUR: ADAPTABILITY

CHAPTER FIVE: SHAME OF PARENT

CHAPTER SIX: SELF-CARE

CHAPTER SEVEN: TANTRUMS

CHAPTER EIGHT: RIVALRY BETWEEN SIBLINGS

CHAPTER NINE: INTOLERANCE FOR FRUSTRATION

CHAPTER TEN: POSSESSING POSITIVE SELF-ESTEEM

CHAPTER ELEVEN: PERFECTIONISM

CHAPTER TWELVE: SEPARATION ANXIETY DISORDER (SAD)

CONCLUSION

INTRODUCTION

Many parents place a strong emphasis on their kids' academic performance and extracurricular involvement. Examples of this include making sure kids study, complete their homework, and arrive on time for dance or soccer practice. However, we frequently overlook the equally vital—if not more so—nurturing of another aspect of a child's success and development, which is being a decent person.

It's easy to overlook how crucial it is to combat the ubiquitous messages of consumerism, selfishness, and instant gratification that permeate our culture.

We can assist in guiding our children toward routines and actions that foster virtues like kindness, generosity, and empathy for those who are less fortunate or in need of assistance if we want to raise truly nice people.

In the words of the late great C.S. Lewis, "Integrity is doing the right thing, even when no one is watching."

How can we bring up a good child—one that will act morally even in the absence of witnesses and without the possibility of reward?

CHAPTER ONE

INCREDIBLY NICE

We are generous, loving, and compassionate people at our core. Believing that children and their parents are good enables us to view behavior, especially during trying or emotionally charged situations, as an expression of needs rather than a person's identity.

Our children are more likely to have empathy for their struggles when we tell them, "You're a good kid having a hard time. I'm here, I'm right here with you." This helps them regulate and make better decisions in the future. To be clear, just because we think well of our children does not mean that we approve of the way they behave.

Being deeply good-hearted toward our children actually enables us to act simultaneously with parental authority, firm boundaries, and tender compassion.

I can explain what Good Parenting is and how it might be related to "Gentle Parenting," though

I'm not exactly sure what that means. Good parenting assumes that everyone is using the resources available to them as best they can. With this perspective, we see children who struggle as good kids going through a difficult period rather than as bad kids doing bad things. This changes the way we approach intervention, rather than punishing behavior, we now focus on developing skills to influence behavior.

There's a misconception that addressing children's emotional needs is "soft," but this couldn't be further from the truth. Since feelings come before thoughts, emphasizing feelings is a sensible, useful, and efficient way to assist people with the source of their problems.

Seeing our children as profoundly good does not mean that we approve of their behavior. Boundaries, restrictions, and jobs are key components of good parenting, for both parents and children.

Additionally, we teach parents how to respect and empathize with their children while exercising authority over them.

The best part is that we think you can be two things: you can be kind and orderly, you can be strong and warm, and you can establish boundaries and show empathy.

When a child is thrashing around on the floor and screaming, a parent may say, "You're a good kid having a hard time. I'll come get you and take you somewhere more sedate. You are not under threat. I'm going to remain by your side so that the two of us can unwind."

CHAPTER TWO

YOIR OBLIGATIONS AND RIGHTS

Children have the right to education, healthcare, safety, affectionate treatment, and protection from abuse and cruelty. Up until the time that a child is old enough to navigate the world on their own, parents have a responsibility to defend their rights.

"Parental responsibility" refers to the power to decide issues that impact the child's care, welfare, and appropriate development.

According to the Family Law Act, the only individuals who have "innate parental responsibility"—that is, the legal right to exercise parental responsibility without a court order—are birth parents, adoptive parents, people who become parents through artificial conception or surrogacy, and those who satisfy presumptions of parentage.

Even though other adults, like stepparents, may assist and care for a child, only these parents—

or those recognized as parents by the court—
have the final say in matters pertaining to the
child.

Your responsibilities don't stop with a divorce or
separation; they last until your child turns 18
years old. Even in cases of separation, the state
and the courts encourage both parents to
participate in the exercise of their parental
responsibilities for a child.

You have rights too as a parent. Parents are
legally permitted to raise their children in
accordance with their own morals and
ideologies. When a child's well-being is in
jeopardy—for instance, when there is abuse or
the child is not receiving the required medical
care or education—decisions about religion,
education, discipline, medical care, and where
the child lives won't be changed.

Working parents are entitled to childcare
services and information about the benefits and
services they can receive.

The idea of parents' rights, however, does not
encompass the right to custody or contact with

your kids, for instance, following a divorce. The law mandates that the child's best interests always come first in circumstances where parental responsibility may be modified.

Making sure your child is attractive to others by the time they turn four is another crucial but often overlooked parental duty.

This is why, if you give it some serious thought, it's simple. Assume for a moment that your child is three years old, or roughly halfway through the early stages of socialization. You also bring that youngster out in public. Okay, so tell me what you want for the kid? The child should be able to socialize with both adults and other kids so that the former will greet him or her with a smile and want to play, and the latter will be delighted to see the child and treat him or her well.

You're throwing the child out into a world where every single face they see is either hostile or lying if your child has turned into a horrible little monster because you're afraid to discipline them or you don't know how to do it properly. All they will experience is rejection from other kids and fake smiles from other parents and adults. Neither your child's mental health nor overall well-being will benefit much from that.

When your child learns a few basic social skills, such as not interrupting adults when they're talking too much, paying attention, and trying not to hit other kids over the head with the truck more often than absolutely necessary, in addition to sharing and playing appropriately, the other kids will try out some small play routines on them when they meet other kids, and that will go smoothly. After that, they'll go off and socialize with each other for the rest of their lives.

The children who fall behind at first, are dropped by their peers and are ostracized and excluded from their peer group for the duration of their lives. They are the ones who develop into long-term antisocial adults.

Although raising children is regarded as one of the hardest jobs in the world, there is no official training program available to teach parents how to do it well. The good news is that there are lots

of ways for parents to engage their infants'
minds and turn ordinary occurrences into
extraordinary educational opportunities.

The director of the documentary Brain Matters,
Carlota Nelson, offers five simple, practical, and
scientifically supported strategies that will help
position your child for success in the future.

1. Encourage infantile speech and regard it as a genuine dialogue

Although a baby's sounds and gestures may not
seem like much, they are their only means of
communication. According to experts in early
childhood development, we should encourage
baby talk and regard it as legitimate dialogue.
Parents should interact with their babies
throughout the day by responding to their
sounds, cues, and actions. The number of words
in a child's vocabulary at age two and their
reading levels later in life is determined by the
number of words to which the baby is exposed.
Baby babble should be encouraged and taken
seriously.

2. Read aloud to your child to practice language

Even though they can't read or talk yet, babies are eager to learn from birth. They are able to identify every sound used in every language in the world, even at the age of three months. Each time you read aloud to your infant, you are helping them develop their language skills. Make sure to ask questions about the plot and the characters, as well as to point to the pictures in the book. Your child's language skills will be stimulated by asking simple questions like "What are they wearing?" and "How many are there?" Reading to infants cultivates a love of books in them. Leaders are readers, remember, so why not get started early?

3. Turn ordinary encounters into educational opportunities

For infants, every experience in life is an opportunity to learn. Bath time, laundry, cooking, and running errands are all excellent opportunities for learning. Explain your language-stimulating activities. To teach math, count and sort laundry, encourage scientific thinking, and experiment with food ingredients and textures. Empathic face-making is an excellent method for teaching emotional intelligence.

4. Play with intention

Young children are constantly learning new things. Playing helps them develop vital life skills. They can learn about other people's emotions and experience what it's like to be in a relationship through pretend play. Playing with others teaches them to share and make concessions.

Playing imaginatively, such as making up a scenario in which a toy train can travel through space, encourages children to express themselves verbally and creatively. Young children are developing their ability to solve problems and think of new possibilities when they imagine new worlds. What appears to be leisure time is actually extremely important work. Play is serious learning, so take it seriously. Refrain from using your device excessively in front of your child. That, according to research, makes kids feel less significant.

5. Set a good example

Infants impersonate geniuses. They become aware of everything you do. They learn to mimic others' expressions and nonverbal cues until they can speak for themselves. Babies pick up on their attitudes and behaviors by observing their body language, how they interact with others, and how they respond to challenges.
Your behavior with your child influences who they grow up to be.

By incorporating these five essential behaviors into your daily routine, you can significantly increase your baby's chances of future success.

The YMCA commissioned OnePoll to survey 2,000 parents, looking at the most important life lessons and mantras that parents want to instill in their kids as well as the obstacles many face along the way, including time, money, and—surprisingly—zip codes.

Financial and practical obstacles were apparent for parents who felt they hadn't been able to teach their kids everything they wanted to. The most common excuses given were being overworked (33 percent), having to prioritize taking care of their family (23 percent), and not having enough time to spend with their kids (22 percent).

It has nothing to do with money or ostentatious learning materials to provide your child with the best tools for future success. It is entirely related to you, your schedule, and your degree of organization. In a recent survey, American parents expressed their desire to teach their children three key life lessons: "honesty is the best policy," "be respectful," and "be thankful for what you have." "Never give up" and "learn from your mistakes" round out the top five life lessons that parents should instill in their children.

CHAPTER THREE

IT'S BETTER LATE THAN NEVER!

Parenting does not have to be characterized by difficult times. Try not to be too hard on yourself. Recall there are no manuals for parenting. Additionally, while some other parents might offer you guidance, it's not always reliable.

So once more, try not to be too hard on yourself and focus on the achievements you have made. Your child will always love you, although they might be passing too much judgment.

Children are constantly evolving and changing. You can talk to someone who is ten years old about your mistakes, which makes it an ideal age to regroup. Own up to them and explain why those actions were ineffective. You can adjust and they will adjust as well, feeling more connected to you and appreciating direct communication. Try it before they hit puberty. Life then becomes more intricate and emotional.

"Am I a bad parent?" This is a rhetorical question we've all end up asking ourselves after an especially trying day. It's common to believe that your parenting abilities are lacking. In moments like these, when nothing seems to be working out for you and you've run out of patience, it's easy to feel like a bad parent. However, the fact that you're questioning whether you're parenting your children well indicates that you're not a bad parent at all.

There are moments when it seems like every error we make is huge and every decision we make is important. We are concerned about how our decisions will affect our children down the road, particularly when it comes to unfavorable interactions.

We worry about whether we should have handled that tantrum better, if we should have yelled at them earlier, or if we applied the proper sanctions. We become so consumed by worry about it that we begin to feel like horrible parents.

However, all parents experience moments of losing their temperament. Everybody has, in a fit of rage or uncertainty, chosen to parent poorly at some point. None of us are bad parents as a result.

What Constitutes Bad Parenting?

Bad parents make poor choices that are not optimal for their kids. Being a good parent doesn't require you to always put your kids' needs ahead of your own.

Certain things are well known to us as being "bad". The most severe and detrimental behavioral characteristics that the majority of us associate with poor parenting are physical abuse, neglect, emotional abuse, and sexual abuse. These are issues that need to be resolved right away with expert assistance.

In addition to intentional and inadvertent child abuse and neglect, parents can also have unintended negative effects on their children through their actions or words. You may feel better about your parenting if you can identify whether you're doing those things.

It's not always simple to evaluate your parenting style honestly. It's crucial to first distinguish the behavior from the individual because of this. It's not appropriate to label someone as a "bad parent" just because you or they have different parenting philosophies or approaches.

It's also critical to understand the distinction between being a bad parent and simply having a bad day. The majority of parents exhibit both positive and negative parenting traits, despite disagreements about what constitutes "good" or "bad" parenting.

What Telltale Signs Indicate Bad Parenting?

When you look at the extremes, it's simple to identify parenting practices that are less than ideal.

- **Too much or too little involvement**

  On one extreme lies the detached parent who is callous and disregards their child's needs beyond providing them with clothing, food, and shelter.

  An overly involved parent, also known as a "helicopter parent," can do more harm than good by taking charge of decisions and going above and beyond for their child, which prevents them from learning by doing. This approach is less harmful than neglectful parenting.

- **Insufficient or nonexistent discipline**

  Children who have little or no discipline are left to fend for themselves, which can lead to injuries and also create a child who does not understand boundaries, claims psychotherapist Sharron Frederick, LCSW, of Clarity Health Solutions. "Children look to parents to define what boundaries are and the consequences that can occur if the child crosses the boundaries," she says.

- **Severe or inflexible rules**

  Frederick claims that parents who enforce strict or rigid discipline, also known as authoritarian parenting, prevent their child from exploring the outside world, which frequently results in a child who grows up fearful, anxious, or rebellious. This is different from parents who enforce little to no discipline.

- **Disgrace**

  Relentless shame of children can lead to problems with perfection and a fear of failing, whether in public or private. Anxiety or depression may result from this.

What Consequences Arise From Poor Parenting?

Negative outcomes such as depression, anxiety, aggression, and relationship problems themselves are more likely in children who do not receive positive parenting. The consequences listed below are the outcome of persistently bad behavior patterns. A one-time incident of physical abuse or a pattern of continuous criticism is not the same as when you yelled at your toddler for smashing your favorite coffee mug.

- **Negative opinion of oneself**

  Overuse of labels and shame is a parenting mistake that can have long-term effects. Shame is a strong, paralyzing emotion that seeps into a person's identity and psyche. Long-term, those who have low self-esteem frequently look for relationships that will confirm the messages they already hear.

- **Problems with control and rebellion**

  Excessively strict or rigid discipline can lead to anxious behaviors, Obsessive-Compulsive Disorder (OCD), difficulties controlling others, and a fearful belief that there is danger in the world.

  The disobedient child, on the other hand, is at the other end of the spectrum. They engage in bad behaviors, fight with their parents, and break the rules.

- **Behavioral and emotional issues**

  A child may experience emotional and behavioral problems, such as aggression and difficulty following instructions at school, as a result of harsh parenting, which includes frequent yelling, hitting, and verbal or physical threats in addition to immediate negative consequences for a particular behavior.

How Can Bad Parenting Be Stopped?

Negative parenting practices can endanger children. Children who experience behavioral or emotional problems can be raised by parents who practice positive discipline and positive interaction techniques. Doing the best you can does not guarantee that your child will never struggle or have issues, just as having one terrible day does not make you a bad parent. Being a parent is a continuous and sometimes difficult process. It could feel even more difficult if you've struggled because of your own parents' less-than-ideal modeling. However, you can make an effort to get past the damaging lessons you were given and create a positive bond with your kids.

Even though your parents weren't the best role models for you, you can still forge your parenting path with the help and encouragement of other parents.

Remember that you are capable of changing if you frequently find yourself slipping into poor parenting practices.

It can take a lot of effort, patience, and honesty to revamp your parenting style. The good news is that it is never too late to get started. Any constructive adjustment you make can benefit your child in the long run.

Here are some pointers to keep your attention on the good.

- **Assign suitable penalties**

  It's important to use discipline, but also to make sure your child learns a valuable lesson. Use a rewards system instead, or make them earn time for enjoyable activities. When taking something away from your child, don't take it away for a week, instead take ist away for the afternoon. Verify that the punishment is appropriate for the behavior you're trying to change.

- **Be devoted and loving.**

  Telling your child that you love them is not the only way to show them your affection and love. It also results from spending quality time with your child, being physically affectionate, and encouraging and accepting them.

- **Allow them to make errors**

  Allow your kids to experiment with creativity and make mistakes because life is messy and you won't judge or shame them for it. Ask your child, "How can you correct this mistake?" after they make one. Make the most of your mistakes to demonstrate to them that learning never ends and that bad days can happen to everyone. Everyone benefits from owning up to mistakes, offering an apology, and making an effort to do better.

CHAPTER FOUR

ADAPTABILITY

Although we often picture childhood as a carefree period, many children experience emotional pain, difficulties, and trauma during their youth. Children may be asked to cope with issues that range from difficulties at home or with peer bullying to adjusting to a new classroom or online learning environment. Childhood can be anything but carefree when you factor in the uncertainties that come with growing up in a complex world. Resilience skills are what allow one to flourish despite these obstacles. It's possible to acquire resilience skills, which is good news.

Children who possess resilience are better able to overcome obstacles, overcome hardship, and grow into emotionally mature adults.

Developing resilience in our kids can help them cope with stress and feelings of anxiety and uncertainty. Resilience is the capacity to bounce back from setbacks, trauma, tragedies, threats, and even major sources of stress. Being resilient does not, however, guarantee that kids won't run into problems or feel upset. When we experience significant trauma or a personal loss, or even hear about someone else's loss or trauma, we frequently experience emotional pain, sadness, and anxiety.

To help kids develop resilience:

- **Remain optimistic and keep things in perspective**

  Encourage your child to maintain a long-term perspective and consider the situation from a wider angle, even when they are experiencing extremely traumatic events.

  Help your child understand that there is a future beyond the present circumstances and that it can be positive, even though they may be too young to think about taking a long-term look on their own. Children who have an upbeat and optimistic mindset can find the good things in life and persevere through the most difficult times. Show them that obstacles and failures are chances for development and education.

- **Help them with promoting an optimistic self-image**
  Assist your child in recalling how they overcame adversity in the past and in realizing that these experiences fortify them to face difficulties in the future. Encourage your child to develop self-confidence in their ability to solve problems and make wise choices.

- **Establish links**
  Instill in your kids the value of interacting and establishing a connection with their peers through honest dialogue, attentive listening, and empathy. Look for ways to support kids in developing connectivity by advising them to make in-person or virtual

connections with peers via text, phone, and video chat. Making connections with people develops resilience, and also offers social support. The development of a solid family network is also crucial. Create a nurturing and encouraging atmosphere, and Give them affection, compassion, and steady emotional support.

- **Continue with your daily schedule**
Children, especially younger ones who need structure in their lives, can find comfort in routine. Together, you should create a schedule that includes appointed times for schoolwork and play. You may need to be adaptable to certain routines, especially during difficult or transitional times. Schedules and regularity must be maintained at the same time.

- **Promote prudent risk-taking**
Encourage them to venture outside of their comfort zones, take on age-appropriate

challenges, and try new things. This taught them important lessons about tenacity and flexibility.

- **Take a rest**

  Although a certain amount of anxiety can spur us to action, we must also acknowledge and accept all emotions. Show your kids how to concentrate on things they can influence or take action on. Encourage them to consider the likelihood of the worst-case scenario and what they might say to a friend who is experiencing similar concerns to help them overcome their unrealistic fears. Keep an eye out for potentially upsetting content your child is exposed to, whether it comes from the news, online, or by listening in on conversations.

CHAPTER FIVE

SHAME OF PARENT

In the natural world, there is only one main, underlying cause that compels parents to intentionally mistreat their children. Although there are other causes, none are as strong as this one.

It might also not be what you believe. The main contributing factors are not anger, depression, a need for control, self-absorption, or demands for (near) perfection; rather, they are responses to the primary reason rather than the one underlying major cause, which comes later in the chain. What then is the reason?

SHAME.

Parental shame is typically what I find at the core of troubled families when I peel back the layers of symptoms and side effects. Parental shame that hasn't been addressed is what drives extreme family dysfunction, including a great deal of stress, conflict, rage, withdrawal, and depression.

Parents will do anything to keep from being overcome by their shame, which they keep hidden and refuse to face. Additionally, there are a lot of ways for kids to inadvertently trigger their parents' shame defense mechanisms and tap into their shame.

How Can Kids Inadvertently Cause and Intensify Parental Guilt?

- **By being small and exhibiting the typical demands for care, love, and affection that children have by nature**

  The child's needs may coincide with the parent's unfulfilled attachment needs, which may make the parent feel extremely threatened. For instance, a preschooler cries because they need after falling off a trike and getting scraped up, to be seen, heard, and comforted could trigger the same unfulfilled needs in his father, needs the father feels ashamed and unmanly in himself, which could result in an angry outburst. "Are you crying over that? That is insignificant. I'll give you something to cry about if you don't stop crying!" The father gets annoyed to protect himself from the guilt of his own unfulfilled needs and the fact that he was and still is so occasionally neglected, hurt, and afraid.

- **By behaving in a way that their parents believe makes them look bad to the outside world**

Occasionally, I witness young children sitting motionless for a full hour during Mass alongside their guardians, Being "very good" at all times rather than fidgeting or wriggling, and it breaks my heart when people tell those parents that. When I consider the cost of that degree of control, I wonder if they were informed that God is angry with kids who fidget in the pew during church. The unresolved shame that parents feel from others about their parenting destabilizes them. Some parents overcontrol their children's behavior, not for the benefit of the child but rather to protect their delicate self-esteem from being threatened by real or perceived criticism from others, which triggers shame.

It is extremely difficult for parents to see their children when they are carrying unresolved shame that could potentially resurface. They shift from relating to one another to defending themselves.

How many people worldwide go hungry because their basic attachment needs aren't being met? How many people are so estranged? so cut off from affection and care?

This is not an attempt to remove shooters' moral responsibility by waving a psychological wand. Here, sin is present. That is beyond my doubt. However, I agree with St. Thomas Aquinas that sin is an attempt to pursue a perceived good that is misguided and maladaptive.

Strategies to Lessen Parental Guilt and Foster Closer Relationships

- **Ignore their depressing attitudes**

  If your child is acting out, try not to get upset or angry with them because that will make the situation worse. Rather, disregard the negativity.

- **Face down negativity with optimism**

  Children will occasionally act out in an attempt to get attention. Your child will probably get upset with you if you constantly complain about everything. However, you have to prevent that from happening. Instead of yelling, use civil discourse and remain composed and kind. They will stop acting in that way as soon as they realize it is not working.

- **Pinpoint the underlying reason**

  You will have a far greater chance of making things better if you can identify the cause of your child's bad behavior. Your child's usual crankiness in the morning may stem from exhaustion. Change his bedtime to prevent him from oversleeping and from waking up exhausted.

- **Teach them how to keep their emotions in check**

  Children may react extremely negatively to rejection or unfavorable circumstances if they do not know how to handle them. By encouraging them to engage in their favorite pastime as a means of relieving stress, you can teach them how to manage their emotions.

- **Take their focus elsewhere**

  Children's short attention spans cause them to frequently become sidetracked by the things they are fussing over. Instead of caving into their pleading, find something acceptable to divert your attention.

- **Encourage positive thinking**

  With your children, you can engage in the "unfortunately/fortunately" game. Put a few cards with unfortunate situations written on them and mix them up in a bowl. Ask your child to read the unfortunate situation on one card that they pulled out. Your child will then need to come up with an additional "fortunately" for it. This will encourage your child to behave in an upbeat manner.

The ability to overcome parental shame is one gift from the natural world that I hope every parent would give their kids. It would be up to each mother to truly undertake her healing and human formation. Each father would have to deal with his unresolved trauma and come to terms with ordered self-love. for fathers and mothers to look for and obtain the support they require to become far more resilient.

Being raised by parents who are comparatively free from the burdens of disordered shame is a rare and beautiful thing. And that's a gift that will endure for many generations. Similar to how controlling, irrational, distant, and other behaviors motivated by parental shame transfer the shame from parents to their offspring, dealing with shame becomes so "normal" that offspring don't understand what healthy relationships and ordered self-love are, instead, they believe it's normal for them to have to shield their parents from the shame of their parents, shame for not feeling comfortable and safe, shame at not being acknowledged, understood, heard, or seen.

Some parents are reluctant to take a close look at their parenting because they are worried about what it might mean for their kids' welfare. They are also worried about what they might discover if they take a serious look at how their parenting is affecting their kids. Parents who are prepared to end the shame cycle that spans generations are desperately needed in our society. who are prepared to take a stand and say yes to their recovery and development as human beings.

CHAPTER SIX

SELF-CARE

As a parent, you may feel like you have to put your children's needs before your own, but you're wrong. Your needs are as important as your children's. Self-care is super important, it is not a luxury—it's a necessity. Emotional activities like practicing gratitude, mindfulness, compassion, and forgiveness are also part of taking care of oneself. Also, don't overlook spiritual practices like praying, meditation, and spending time in nature.

Self-care is not conceitful or frivolous. It's not about running away from your duties or ignoring your kids. Taking care of yourself is an important factor in becoming the best parent you can be. It's about looking after yourself so that you can better look after other people. It's about having something to pour out of by first filling up your cup.

Engaging in self-care activities can help you take better care of your children. Making your health a priority gives you the energy, tolerance, and emotional fortitude to tackle the difficulties of parenthood. It assists you in keeping your needs and your child's needs in a healthy balance.

By practicing self-care, you can reduce stress, improve your mental health, and enhance your overall happiness, which ultimately contributes to being a better parent

How Self-Care Benefits You and Your Children?

Self-care has many benefits for both you and your children. Here are some of them:

- Self-care can help you replenish your energy, focus, and positivity.
- Self-care can help you cope with stress.
- Self-care can help you prevent burnout.
- You can teach your kids healthy habits by practicing self-care.

How a Parent Can Take Care of theirself?

It can be difficult to practice self-care as a parent at first, but it doesn't have to be difficult or time-consuming. Exotic trips and pricey spa treatments are not necessary (though those are also quite nice). All you need are a few easy tactics that fit into your daily schedule and work for you.

Negative self-care, or the lack of self-care, can have a detrimental effect on parenting. When parents neglect their well-being and constantly put their needs aside, it can result in burnout, exhaustion, and increased stress levels. This can result in decreased patience, irritability, and difficulty in managing emotions, which can negatively impact the parent-child relationship. Moreover, when parents don't prioritize self-care, they may struggle to maintain a healthy work-life balance, leading to less quality time spent with their children. This can affect the overall emotional connection and bonding between parent and child. Additionally, neglecting self-care can also set a poor example for children. They learn from their parents' behaviors and actions, so if they see their parents constantly stressed and not taking care of themselves, they may internalize the belief that self-care is not important.

Negative self-care can, in general, have a knock-on effect on parenting that impacts the relationship between parents and children as well as the parents' well-being. Prioritizing self-care is crucial for parents if they want to be the best versions of themselves for their kids.

Never forget that you have just as much right to self-care as you do for the rest of your family. You will enhance your well-being and that of your children by engaging in regular self-care.

CHAPTER SEVEN

TANTRUMS

A tantrum is a frequently immature outburst of rage. When your child "loses it," they may result in spectacular outbursts of rage, frustration, and disorganized behavior.

This is because the social, emotional, and linguistic development of young children is still in its infancy. They may become frustrated because they find it difficult to express their needs, feelings, and desire to take care of themselves. They are also learning that their actions have an impact on other people. Thus, throwing tantrums is one way that young children try to make sense of or alter the world around them, as well as express and manage their feelings.

Even older kids can throw fits. This might be the result of their lack of experience with safe emotional expression and management.

Why Do Children Throw Fits?

Children may throw tantrums when they are uncomfortable, hungry, or tired. When they can't get what they want (like a toy or candy) or can't get someone to do what they want (like getting a sibling to give up the tablet or getting a parent to pay attention to them right away), they can have a meltdown. Children gradually develop the ability to handle frustration.

A frustrating experience may result in a tantrum in toddlers because they are not always able to express what they need or want and because words that describe feelings are more complex and develop later. Tantrums usually become less common as language abilities advance.

Toddlers are overly ambitious for independence and control over their surroundings. Power struggles may result from a child believing that "I can do it myself" or "I want it, give it to me." Kids may throw a tantrum when they realize they can't accomplish everything and can't have everything they desire.

How Can Tantrums Be Prevented?

Whenever possible, try to stop tantrums before they start. The following suggestions might be useful:

- **Pay close attention to everything positive**

  Make it a habit to recognize your child's good behavior. Give your child attention and praise when they behave well. Express precisely what actions you would like to see more frequently when praising them (e.g., "I appreciate how you waited for your milk and said please," or "Thank you for sharing the blocks with your sister").

- **Give toddlers some control over small objects, if possible**

  Rather than arguing with your child over a mismatched outfit, for instance, think about whether this could be a chance to promote independence and self-expression and whether it matters given the schedule for the day. Off-limits items should be kept hidden and out of reach. Conflicts are less likely as a result. Of course, this isn't always feasible, particularly in uncontrollable environments like those outside the home.

- **Take your child's attention elsewhere**
  Instead of giving them what they can't have, try giving them something else. Instead of engaging in the annoying or prohibited activity, start a new one (For instance, offer your child a plastic container and wooden spoon and ask them to come to help you "cook" if they are jumping on the couch. Instead of having them throw a fit or refuse to get down, you can then commend them for helping or listening to instructions. or just alter the surroundings. Take your young child into

the house, outdoors, or into a different room.

- **Encourage children to thrive and pick up new skills**

  Aid children in their learning. Give them compliments to make them feel good about their abilities. Additionally, begin with a basic task before advancing to more difficult ones.

  When your child makes a request, carefully consider what they are asking for. Is that out of the ordinary? Perhaps it isn't. Pick your battles. If you initially said no, it's perfectly acceptable to change your mind. Just make sure to find a way to reward good behavior by allowing the desired treat.

- **Recognize your kids' boundaries**

  It's not the ideal time to go grocery shopping or attempt to fit in one more errand if you know your toddler is exhausted. Like adults, hungry kids are more likely to ask for food in the store than kids who have just eaten.

How Should I Respond to a Tantrum?

- **When responding to a tantrum, maintain your composure**

  Avoid adding to the issue by letting your annoyance or rage get in the way. Remember that your role is to assist your child in developing self-control. Thus, you too must maintain your composure.

  The way you respond to a tantrum will vary depending on your child's cause of upset. You might occasionally need to offer consolation. It's time for a snack or nap if your child is feeling hungry or exhausted. At other times, it's best to ignore your child's outburst or divert their attention to something else.

- **Ignoring a tantrum that is being thrown to get attention from parents is one of the best ways to stop it**

  Refrain from giving your child a lot of explanations for why they can't have what they want if your child throws a tantrum after being denied something. Proceed to a different task with your youngster. It's advisable to ignore a tantrum that your child throws if they are told to do something they don't want to do. However, make sure you have your child finish the assignment once they're calm.

- **Do not give in to your child's tantrum**

  The reason is, if you do, you've actually proved to your child that tantrum is effective. Try making a "chill out" spot in your home. The spot should have a soft cushion, books, calming music and other relaxing activities. And the place should be a place where others won't disturb the child. Motivate your child to go to the spot when annoyed, to learn to relax and control frustration.

When Should I Call the Doctor?

Talk to your doctor if:
- You often feel angry or out of control when you respond to tantrums.
- You keep giving in to try to avoid your child acting out.
- The tantrums cause a lot of bad feelings between you and your child or you and your partner.
- The tantrums happen frequently, or last longer
- Someone is harmed in the heat of the moment, be it your child or others.
- Your child seems very disagreeable, argues a lot, and hardly ever cooperates.

CHAPTER EIGHT

RIVALRY BETWEEN SIBLINGS

The common phrase "sibling rivalry" refers to the continuous hostility between children raised in the same household. It can happen between siblings who are related by blood, step-siblings, adopted siblings, or foster siblings.

During childhood, siblings commonly spend more time together than with their parents. The sibling bond is frequently complex and impacted by people and experiences outside of the family, personality traits, birth order, and parental treatment, among other things. When children are of the same gender and age, or when one or more of the children are gifted intellectually, sibling rivalry is especially strong.

Judith Dunn's observational studies indicate that children become sensitive to variations in their parents' treatment as early as one year of age. Siblings can comprehend family rules and know how to console and treat each other with kindness starting at 18 months of age. By the time they are three years old, kids have a firm understanding of social norms, can assess their worth in comparison to their siblings, and can adjust to changes in the family environment.

Sibling rivalry can be extremely upsetting and stressful for parents and frequently lasts throughout childhood. Teenagers fight for the same reasons that younger kids fight, but they are more capable of inflicting physical, psychological, and emotional harm on one another as well as being physically, psychologically, and emotionally harmed themselves. The teenage years are stressful because of changes in one's physical and emotional makeup as well as in one's interactions with friends and parents. The likelihood of fighting with siblings to gain attention from parents may rise during adolescence. According to one study, siblings competed at the highest level between the ages of 10 and 15.

Sibling rivalry can persist into adulthood, and over time, sibling relationships can undergo significant transformations. Siblings may become closer as a result of circumstances like a parent's illness, but marriage may drive them apart, especially if there is tension in the in-law relationship. About one-third of adults say they have a competitive or aloof relationship with their siblings. Rivalry, though, usually wanes with time. Among siblings over 60, at least 80% have close relationships.

Every child in a family competes to define who he is as an individual and wants to demonstrate that he is different from their siblings, according to Kyla Boyse of the University of Michigan. Youngsters may believe they are receiving different levels of their parents' responsiveness, attention, and discipline. Children fight most in families where there is no alternative method of handling conflicts or understanding that fighting is not an acceptable way to resolve them. In families where physical fighting is Prohibited, but no non-physical dispute resolution technique (like verbal sparring) is allowed, the transformation and build-up of daily disagreements into simmering animosities can have an impact almost as damaging. Stress in the lives of parents and kids can exacerbate rivalry between siblings and lead to more arguments.

Alternative Psychological Strategies

According to Alfred Adler, personality development is significantly influenced by birth order, with siblings perceived as "striving for significance" within the family. Age, gender, and birth order all have an impact on sibling relationships, according to psychologists and researchers today. On the other hand, parents are thought to have a significant impact on whether or not their children are competitive.

According to David Levy, who coined the term "sibling rivalry" in 1941, "the aggressive response to the new baby is so typical that it is safe to say it is a common feature of family life for the older sibling".Today's researchers largely support this perspective, pointing out that parents can lessen this reaction by being aware of favoritism and by taking the necessary precautions. The months leading up to the new baby's arrival are the best time to establish the foundation for a lifetime of supportive relationships between siblings.

Parenting Approach

Sibling relationships are influenced by parents. Many aspects of the parent-child relationship can then be incorporated into the sibling connection. How their parents raised them influences how the skills and interests of the siblings differ.

According to Jensen and McHale (2015), "Although they are 50% genetically similar, on average, and usually grow up in the same home, full biological siblings are typically no more similar to one another than they are to strangers". These differences affect the child's perception of themselves about the wider family dynamic. A child's perception of their position in the family is influenced by the early classifications made by their parents. Sibling differentiation research and Adler's psychology theory both suggest that siblings differ from one another to address specific needs in the family and reduce conflict and competition for family resources. Siblings are expected to gradually diverge from one another as a result of this mechanism.

Research indicates that when children have higher expectations for their future accomplishments, they often live up to their parents' expectations. This could result in parental treatment of siblings differing. Research has shown that a lot of parents place greater value on their daughters than on their sons, and this affects the birth order. The oldest child is also expected to perform to the highest standards in many families. This difference in opinions about a child's chances of success can result in physical and emotional isolation, neglect, and bias.

Youngsters are impacted by the treatment of their siblings that they observe their parents providing. Youngsters who witness violent parent-child interactions or who are subjected to abuse and strict parenting are more likely to react violently toward their siblings.

Coercion theory holds that hostile, coercive sibling interactions arise from poor parenting (e.g., using harsh punishments like spanking or scolding) and neglecting to discipline a child. Parents interaction with their children affects their behaviour with others. Inadequate child supervision and parent-child hostility have been linked to higher rates of aggression in children.

Another parenting behavior that is related to the quality of the sibling connection is the sibling relationship, which reflects more warmth and less animosity between parents and children. Children's interactions with others are greatly influenced by the way their parents interact with each other. Family contact patterns have the greatest influence on children's socialization during childhood, as opposed to other life stages. Sibling relationships, which are among the most enduring, can aid in children's cognitive and socioemotional development.

A parent's parenting style can have a detrimental effect on a child's future relationships with other people as well as their relationship with their siblings. While some sibling rivalry is unavoidable, this does not indicate that your parenting style or your kids are flawed. By avoiding comparisons and stereotyping their kids, organizing enjoyable family activities, and ensuring that each child has enough time and space to themselves, parents can lessen the likelihood of rivalry.

In addition, they can avoid showing favoritism, give each child their undivided attention, promote teamwork, and refuse to use one child—say, the oldest—as an example for the others, like the younger ones. It is less likely that kids will turn to forceful attention-getting techniques if they are taught constructive ways to ask for help from their parents when they need it. According to Eileen Kennedy-Moore, parents must also respond to their children's polite, helpful, and inventive pleas for attention to "catch children being good" for this remedy to work.

Additionally, parents can assist their children in resolving conflicts that arise as a normal part of growing up by being proactive in teaching them emotional intelligence, problem-solving techniques, negotiation techniques, and the importance of finding win-win solutions. Sibling rivalry can be further reduced by parents working together to foster bonding over competition.

Organizing family meetings is another method—and among the best—to try to stop sibling rivalry. To foster communication amongst the family members, consider arranging weekly or bimonthly get-togethers. These relaxed get-togethers give siblings a chance to communicate and share their ideas, opinions, and feelings while also helping them to see themselves as a part of the bigger team.

Sylvia Rimm asserts that while sibling rivalry can be lessened, it is unlikely to be completely eradicated. When rivalry is present in healthy amounts, it may be a sign that each child is self-assured enough to voice any disagreements with other siblings.

According to Vernon Weihe, four factors should be taken into consideration when determining whether a behavior is being used for sibling abuse or rivalry. To rule out the possibility that the behavior in question is, in fact, age-appropriate for the child exhibiting it, one must first take into account the fact that children use different conflict-resolution strategies during different developmental stages.

Second, it's important to ascertain if the behavior is a one-time occurrence or a consistent pattern. Abuse is by definition a long-term pattern as opposed to sporadic arguments.

Third, ascertain whether the behavior has an "aspect of victimization"; abuse is typified by secrecy and an unequal power dynamic, whereas rivalry is typically incident-specific, reciprocal, and visible to others.

Fourth, it is important to ascertain the purpose of the questioned and/or dubious behavior. In contrast to rivalry, which is driven solely or mostly by a child's self-interest and does not take into account the interests of others, including the child's rival, abuse situations typically involve the perpetrator's ultimate goals being to dominate, humiliate, or at least cause the victim to feel embarrassed.

Try not to intervene when children argue. Only intervene if there is a risk of bodily harm. Always getting involved runs the risk of causing more issues. Instead of teaching the kids to solve problems on their own, they might begin to expect your assistance and wait for you to show up.

Furthermore, even if you don't mean to, you might give the impression to one child that another is constantly "protected," which could incite even more resentment in them.

Furthermore, because they are constantly being "saved" by a parent, "rescued" children might believe they can get away with more.

It's acceptable to use suitable language to "coach" children through their emotions if you find the language used to be offensive or contain name-calling. This is not the same as stepping in, intervening, or dividing the children.
Encourage them to handle the situation on their own even in that case. If you do intervene, work with your children to solve issues rather than on their behalf.

The following actions are things to think about when participating:

- **Keep children apart until they are quiet** Occasionally, it's preferable to just give them some space and avoid bringing up the argument again. If not, the fight may intensify once more. Wait until the emotions have subsided if you want to use this as a teaching moment. Don't focus too much on determining which child is at fault. Fighting takes two, and each party involved bears some of the blame.

- **Next, make an effort to create a "win-win" scenario where every child benefits**

  When they have the same toy in mind, Instead, maybe they could play a game together. Recall that children who learn how to handle conflict also acquire lifelong lessons such as appreciating the perspectives of others, engaging in constructive dialogue, and managing their violent tendencies.

Simple daily actions that can be taken to avoid fighting include:

- **Establish guidelines for appropriate conduct**

  Advise the children to keep their hands to themselves and to refrain from swearing, calling names, yelling, or slamming doors. Ask them for their opinions on the guidelines and the repercussions for breaking them. This dissuades children from obsessing over who was "right" or "wrong" and instead teaches them that they are accountable for their actions regardless of the circumstance or degree of annoyance. Children should not lead you to believe that everything must always be "fair" and "equal" because there are instances when one child needs more than the other.

- **Spend one-on-one time with your children, attending to their needs and interests**

For instance, if you enjoy being outside, go for a walk or visit a park. Make time for a child who enjoys reading aloud if there is another one. Make sure kids have their own space and time to do their own thing whenever possible. This includes playing with toys alone, playing with friends without a sibling joining in, and enjoying activities without having to split the fun evenly. Teach and demonstrate to your children that love has no bounds to it. Reassure them that their needs will be satisfied and that they are valuable, safe, and loved.

- **Enjoy time spent as a family**

  You are creating a calm environment for your children to interact with one another and spend time together, whether you are playing a board game, throwing a ball, or watching a movie. This keeps you involved and can help reduce their tension. Fun family activities can help reduce conflict because many children fight over their caregiver's attention. If your kids fight frequently over the same things (like video games or who gets to use the TV remote), make a schedule that indicates which kid "owns" what during the week. (But take away the "prize" completely if they continue to fight about it.) If there are frequent fights among your school-age children, schedule weekly family meetings to go over the ground rules regarding fighting and celebrate previous victories in lowering conflict. Establish a system where children can work together to stop fighting and earn points toward a fun family-friendly activity.

- **Acknowledge when children simply require time apart from one another and the dynamics of the family**

Consider setting up separate activities or playdates for each child on occasion. Additionally, you can spend one-on-one time with another child while the other is out for play. Remember that children will occasionally fight for their parents' attention. If that's the case, think about taking a personal break. The reason to fight is gone when you leave. Additionally, if your partner's patience is greater than yours at that particular moment and you find yourself losing your cool, ask them to step in.

When Should I Seek Expert Assistance?

Seldom is sibling rivalry so bad that it interferes with day-to-day activities or negatively impacts children emotionally or psychologically. Under such circumstances, consulting a mental health professional is advisable. Seek assistance for sibling conflict if it poses a genuine risk of bodily harm to any family member, and killis so bad that it's ruining your marriage or relationship.

Seek assistance for sibling conflict if it is detrimental to a family member's psychological health or sense of self-worth and may be linked to other major issues like depression

Consult your physician if you have concerns about the fighting between your children. They can direct you to nearby behavioral health resources and assist you in determining whether

your family would benefit from professional
assistance.

CHAPTER NINE

INTOLERANCE FOR FRUSTRATION

Parents of two and three-year-olds anticipate tantrums and behavioral problems. However, temper tantrums don't always end when a child reaches toddlerhood. It can be difficult to maintain your composure while keeping the peace in such a circumstance.

A normal human emotion is frustration. It's normal for parents to experience occasional feelings of overwhelm and annoyance. But the real question is, is it typical to get frustrated with kids?

The response is overwhelmingly in the affirmative!

It is quite common for parents to become irritated with their kids. Youngsters continue to push boundaries, make mistakes, and learn new things. Their behavior can test a parent's tolerance and make it hard to maintain composure. It's normal for parents to feel overwhelmed, irate, and frustrated when their child consistently misbehaves or disobeys.

But being frustrated does not equate to being a bad parent. It matters how you respond to and communicate these emotions. Parents frequently respond to their children without thinking through the possible consequences. Belittling, hitting, or yelling at kids can lower their self-esteem and negatively impact the parent-child bond over time.

Rather, the key to healthy parenting is learning healthy coping mechanisms for frustration, like deep breathing exercises, taking a break (walking into a different room for a few minutes), or getting help from a psychologist or trusted friend.

Even with our best efforts, we can occasionally lose our patience and become angry with our kids. By owning up to your actions and expressing regret, you can use this as a chance to teach your child valuable life lessons. Consider using this sample script: "I apologize. I was shouting at you because I was upset. I'm sure you were angry when I yelled at you. I cherish you. I'm going to take some deep breaths the next time I feel angry." Here, you've given your kids the chance to witness their parents err, apologize, solve a problem, and come to a resolution.

How Parents Can Control Their Children's Behavior

- **Set limits**

  Controlling misbehavior and lowering the likelihood of becoming frustrated can be accomplished through clearly defining expectations, establishing rules and boundaries, and communicating.

- **Make your emotional health a priority**

  You'll feel more resilient and prepared to face the demanding demands of parenting if you take care of your emotional health and make time for self-care.

- **Look for original methods to communicate**

  Getting along with a child who has a short fuse is difficult. There are imaginative methods to communicate with them, though. Playing games with them, giving them praise, positive reinforcement, and acknowledgment, participating in their favorite activities, providing them with a judgment-free environment, and using humor to lighten the mood will all help you manage their angry behavior as well as your irritation.

- **Encourage children to express their anger**

  Determine the cause of your child's outburst if it is currently occurring. Remind them during the time-out that they are free to express their emotions without acting inappropriately.

  Our goal is to normalize the emotion while changing the behavior.

Remember, just like adults, it takes time for children's emotions to subdue. During this time, try providing a space, a calm tone, and allow the emotions to disperse before questioning. Feeling frustrated with children is normal, and it's a common experience for many parents. The key is recognizing and acknowledging these feelings and finding healthy ways to cope with them. By doing so, parents can provide their children with a positive and supportive environment and build strong and meaningful relationships.

CHAPTER TEN

POSSESSING POSITIVE SELF-ESTEEM

When children feel good about themselves, it's sometimes easy to tell when they don't. Being confident is correlated with having high self-esteem, which is the idea of feeling good about yourself.

Positive self-esteem makes kids feel confident, liked, and accepted. It makes them proud of what they can achieve and think good things about themselves. Children who possess negative self-esteem vehemently scold themselves and question their abilities. They pay lots of attention to their failures than their successes because they believe they are inferior to other children.

What Makes Self-Esteem Important?

Children who are confident in themselves are more willing to try new things and give it their all.

They feel proud of themselves. Self-esteem also helps kids cope with mistakes. They feel motivated to try again, even if they fail at first attempt. Self-esteem helps kids do better at home, at school and with friends.

Kids with low self-esteem feel unsure of themselves. They let others treat them badly and have a hard time standing up for themselves. They give up easily or rather not try at all. Kids with low self-cstccm find it hard to cope when they fail, lose or make a mistake.

How Does One Get Self-Esteem?

When a baby receives loving care and positive attention, self-esteem can begin to develop. It starts when a child experiences acceptance, safety, and love.

Babies can do certain tasks on their own as they grow into toddlers and early children. When they can put their newfound abilities to use, they are happy. When parents give their kids opportunities to try new things, smile, and express pride, it boosts their self-esteem.

When kids get older and try new things, do new things, and learn new things, their self-esteem can always rise. This could occur when children move closer to your objective; learn in class and achieve academic success; form friendships and enjoy common interests in sports, music, art, cooking, and technology;help, give, or show kindness; work hard and receive recognition; feel understood and accepted. Children who feel good about themselves feel competent, confident, and accepted for who they are.

Here are ways you can help your children develop their self-esteem

- **Encourage them to try new things**
  Diversifying their interests is a good thing for kids to do. When they learn new skills, they feel capable and confident that they can handle anything that comes their way.

- **Give them praise for perseverance**
  Learning not to give up easily or quit after one setback is a crucial life skill. Self-esteem and confidence are not about succeeding at everything. They always revolve around having the fortitude to keep trying and not giving up easily when you don't perform to the highest standard.

- **Assist children in discovering their passion**
  Kids can develop a sense of identity through pursuing their interests, and

identity is crucial for boosting confidence. Naturally, witnessing their abilities develop will also greatly enhance their self-worth.

- **Honor hardwork**

  While congratulating children on their achievements is admirable, it's equally critical to express your pride in their efforts to whatever extent they succeed. Learning new skills requires effort, and results aren't always noticeable right away. Whether they are toddlers building with blocks or teenagers learning how to play the guitar on their own, let them know you appreciate the work they are doing.

- **Assume they will assist**

  Even though they may grumble, children who are expected to perform age-appropriate tasks—like tidying up toys, doing dishes, or picking up younger siblings from a playdate—feel more appreciated and connected. While after-school programs and homework are wonderful, it is really important to be needed by your family.

- **Accept your imperfections**

  As adults, we understand that perfection is unachievable, so children must learn this lesson early on. Help children realize that the notion that people are always content, successful, and well-groomed is a destructive fantasy that can be found in media like TV, magazines, and friends' social media feeds. Remind them instead that imperfection is a natural part of humanity and is acceptable.

- **Set them up for success**

  While challenges are good for kids, they also need to have opportunities where they can be sure to succeed. Encourage your child to participate in activities that will help him feel comfortable and confident enough to take on a bigger challenge.

- **Show your love**

Reminding your child that you love him regardless of the outcome of the big game, his grades, or even your anger toward him will boost his self-worth even when he doesn't feel good about himself

CHAPTER ELEVEN

PERFECTIONISM

Perfectionism is another ballpark, it's not an actual diagnosis, but it's also pervasive. It is to be the best that we can be. The problem with it is, it's not rewarding. So perfectionism is about fearing failure.

Understanding Perfectionists Children who have perfectionist tendencies exhibit a continuum of behaviors. These kids experience little joy from perfectionism and a great deal of self-reproach because they believe that mistakes are unacceptable.

It seems that a combination of innate tendencies and external circumstances leads to perfectionism. These can include seeing adults exhibit perfectionist tendencies, receiving excessive praise or demands from parents, teachers, or trainers, and having parental love contingent on the child's exceptional achievement.

Excessive perfectionism has been connected to eating disorders, Obsessive-Compulsive Disorder (OCD), depression, suicide, performance and social anxiety, and migraine headaches. These kids require help when their actions interfere with their socialization and regular development.

Traits of Those Who Strive for Perfection

Extreme perfectionists in children can be identified by several traits, such as:

- Extremely high standards for themselves,
- A tendency to be critical of others,
- Difficulty making decisions and prioritizing tasks,
- Strong feelings of inadequacy and low self-confidence,
- Persistent anxiety about making mistakes,
- Heightened sensitivity to criticism,
- Procrastination and avoidance of stressful situations or difficult tasks,

- Emotional guardedness social inhibition, and

- Headaches or other physical ailments when they perform below expectations of others or themselves.

Children who are gifted and used to performing well are frequently perfectionists. Issues arise when they shy away from taking on new tasks or don't finish their work because it might not be perfect. Children who are gifted but underachievers are the result. If these students try to perform at an exceptional level in every academic subject, they may also become burned out.

How Parents Can Support Their Children's Perfectionism

The following are some ways that parents can support their children who display extreme perfectionism:

- Show respect and care without conditions.

- Establish a serene, orderly, and well-organized atmosphere.
- Do not compare kids.
- Give particular recognition (Effective Praise), Steer clear of terms like genius, brilliant, and flawless.
- Make use of your listening and speaking abilities.
- Children's negative emotions, such as frustration, anxiety, sadness, and fear, should be acknowledged without passing judgment.
- Encourage kids to write in a journal where they can express their ideas and emotions.
- Assist them in realizing that mistakes are inevitable when completing any task.
- Promote high standards while making it clear that excellent work and perfectionism are not the same thing.
- Encourage them to establish reasonable goals for themselves.
- Remind them that they are loved even in the face of failure.

- If someone calls themselves a failure, refute their assertion and offer a more sensible assessment.
- Assist them in setting priorities and dividing larger tasks into smaller, more manageable chunks.
- Instruct them to edit, start over, and grow from their mistakes.
- Rename the objective for those who put things off from perfection to completion.
- If they perform below expectations, offer assistance.
- Assist them in developing coping mechanisms like encouraging "self-talk" (Suggested Thoughts)
- Promote the application of self-control techniques (The Crucial Ability of Restraint)
- Encourage them to practice relaxation techniques like deep breathing, walking, reading, playing a hobby, listening to calming music, counting slowly, and taking deep breaths.

- Read biographies of accomplished individuals who overcame adversity, persisted, and attained greatness, such as Albert Einstein, Helen Keller, and Abraham Lincoln.
- Assist them in realizing that talking badly about themselves is bad for their mental health.
- Provide them with success opportunities to boost their confidence.
- Facilitate positive peer interactions by engaging in a range of activities.
- Give them some practice making nice remarks to other people.
- Meet with their teachers to encourage a collaborative learning environment.
- Own up to your own mistakes.
- Show tenacity in the face of a challenging task.
- When facing setbacks, employ healthy coping mechanisms.

- Evaluate your level of competition and, if needed, lessen the emphasis you place on winning.

Adolescents experiencing severe perfectionism require support from the adults in their lives. They might also require assistance from a licensed therapist. Reducing their perfectionist tendencies to the point where they become a strength rather than a weakness would be the aim.

You may have overheard a parent exclaim with pride, "My son spent all night perfecting his science fair project." He tends to be a perfectionist. However, a parent who views perfectionism as a status symbol is probably unaware of the serious consequences that come with it.

A growing perfectionist may exhibit a variety of behaviors, such as torn papers, late nights, and crying fits, all of which you may have personally witnessed if you're raising a perfectionist.

CHAPTER TWELVE

SEPARATION ANXIETY DISORDER (SAD)

What Is Children's Separation Anxiety Disorder? A particular category of mental health issue is Separation Anxiety Disorder (SAD). When a child has SAD, they frequently worry about being away from their family or other close friends. The youngster fears becoming separated from their family. or, if they are not present, of a family member experiencing something negative.

All young people experience anxiety to some extent. It's a typical aspect of maturing. Anxiety related to separation is common in very young children. Between the ages of 18 months and 3 years, separation anxiety affects almost all kids. However, SAD symptoms are more intense. Unage-appropriate anxieties and fears about being away from home or family plague a child suffering from social anxiety disorder (SAD).

What Leads To A Child's Separation Anxiety Disorder (SAD)?

According to experts, biological and environmental factors contribute to SAD. Anxiety is something that can be inherited by a child. Most likely, there is an imbalance between two chemicals in the brain, serotonin and norepinephrine.

Anxiety and fear can also be taught to a child by other people and family members. SAD can also result from a traumatic incident.

Which Kids Are Most Probably Developing Separation Anxiety Disorder?

Males and females experience SAD equally. However, the likelihood of SAD in children is higher when their parents suffer from anxiety disorders.

What Signs Do Children Have Of Separation Anxiety Disorder?

The first symptoms of SAD usually appear around the 3rd or 4th grade. They may start following a break from school, or after a long-term sickness. Each child may have different symptoms. But the majorly occuring signs of SAD are:

- Refusing to spend the night by themselves
- Nightmares that recur often and center on separation
- Anxiety when away from family or home
- An excessive amount of concern for a family member's safety
- Overly concerned about disappearing from relatives
- Refusing to attend classes
- Fear and aversion to solitude
- Recurring headaches, stomachaches, or other physical discomfort
- Tension or aches in the muscles

- Too much concern for one's safety Too much concern for or when sleeping elsewhere
- Being extremely needy, even at home
- Temper tantrums or panic attacks when away from parents or other caregivers

SAD symptoms can mimic those of other medical conditions. Ensure that your child receives a diagnosis from their medical professional.

How Is A Child's Separation Anxiety Disorder (SAD) Diagnosed?

The doctor who treats your child will perform a physical examination. This is to make sure that your child's symptoms are not due to any physical issues. A child psychiatrist or other mental health professional can diagnose SAD in your child if they don't have any physical health issues. They will evaluate your child's mental health.

Your child's anxiety or fear of being apart from family members needs to persist for at least four weeks for them to be diagnosed with SAD.

Can Separation Anxiety Disorder (SAD) be Treated?

The answer is YES. The following are frequently used in combination with SAD treatment:

- **Cognitive behavioral intervention**
  A child who receives this treatment gains more control over their anxiety. Assisting a child in mastering the circumstances that might trigger anxiety is another objective.

- **Medications**
  Certain children may feel more at ease when taking antidepressant or antianxiety medications.

- **Family counseling**

  In any treatment, parents are extremely important.

- **Contributions from schools**

  The care of a child may also involve the child's school.

How Can I Help My Child Avoid Separation Anxiety Disorder (SAD)?

Experts are unsure of the best ways to stop SAD in kids and teenagers. However, you can assist your child by getting evaluated as soon as possible if you see symptoms of SAD in them. Early intervention can improve your child's typical development and reduce symptoms. It can also raise the standard of living for your child.

What Support Can I Offer My Child When They Have Separation Anxiety Disorder (SAD)?

You, as a parent, are crucial to how your child is treated. The following are some ways you can come in:

- **Observe all of your child's doctor's appointments**

  Don't break the pledges you make to your kids. You will gain your child's trust and independence if you honor your return promise.

- **Give your child brief "away times" to spend with people they can trust**

  For example, having a quick playdate with a friend. Or going to see granny's house.

- **Recognize what circumstances could cause your child stress**

  You can help your child succeed by understanding what stresses them out and making plans for the future.

- **Inform people about your child's SAD**

  Establish a treatment plan in collaboration with the school and your child's medical professional. Inform teachers that there are times when your child will require additional comfort and assistance.

Important Information Regarding Separation Anxiety Disorder (SAD) in Children

- SAD is a specific kind of mental illness. When a child has SAD, they frequently worry about being away from their family or other close friends.

- SAD has environmental and biological causes.
- A diagnosis of SAD should not be made until all other possible causes have been explored.
- When compared to the typical separation anxiety that almost all children experience to some extent between the ages of 18 months and 3 years, symptoms of SAD are more severe.
- For a child to be classified as SAD, their symptoms must persist for at least four weeks.
- To diagnose SAD, a mental health evaluation is required.
- Both counseling and medication are part of the treatment.
- Family therapy and individual therapy for parents may also be beneficial if they are anxious as well.
- Working together with parents and teachers can help the child manage their anxiety.

CONCLUSION

Parenting is an emotionally taxing job. It's also a great responsibility that calls for tolerance, constancy, love, understanding, and compassion. Everybody has days when they question the parenting decisions they made. It's only natural for us to want the best for our children because we adore them so much.

Always keep in mind that you are learning as you go and that you can start over every day. We can all choose to be the kind of parents we want to be if we have the necessary resources and patience for both ourselves and our kids.

Furthermore keep in mind that everyone needs assistance, sometimes more than others. Seek support, direction, advice, and viewpoints from friends, family, coworkers, or mental health professionals you respect and trust if you're feeling overburdened or stretched.

The world's hardest job is being a parent. Keep going; you can do this!